A River Within Spills Light

A River Within Spills Light

Poems by Jane Attanucci

Turning Point

Published by Turning Point
P.O. Box 541106
Cincinnati, OH 45254-1106

ISBN: 9781625493828

Poetry Editor: Kevin Walzer
Business Editor: Lori Jareo

Visit us on the web at www.turningpointbooks.com

Table of Contents

VI

The riverbed dried-up, half-full of leaves.
Us, listening to a river in the trees.

—Seamus Heaney, *The Haw Lantern*, 1987.

I

Perhaps I Should Tell You

I didn't write a single
poem, before my
parents were gone.
Perhaps my good fortune,
their dying young,
leaving me free with my grief.

In my memory
of a dream—
a seal bobs in the shallows
close to shore, while a herd
of others scramble and bark
on a sand bar in the near distance.

Under pale gray skies,
piping plovers roost
in the dunes.
I place my words whole
on the unexpected page,

3725 Frazier Street, 1965

I was the first to smell the smoke.
My brothers and sisters squabbled,
seven 'round the table, giddy bedlam.
So many times we cowered, we cried.

My brothers and sisters squabbled.
Cans of Iron City, forbidden cigarettes.
So many times we cowered, we cried.
And I remember Mom's rage.

Cans of Iron City, forbidden cigarettes.
The oldest girl, I'm alone with the younger ones,
and I remember Mom's rage,
home with diapers, dishes, long division.

The oldest girl, I'm alone with the younger ones,
soot-stained windows, painted bricks,
home with diapers, dishes, long division.
My mother's house still stands.

Soot-stained windows, painted bricks,
the myth is when I left, I never returned.
My mother's house stands still.
O Pittsburgh, my font, my wellspring.

The myth is when I left, I never returned.
Seven 'round the table, giddy bedlam.
O Pittsburgh, my font, my wellspring.
I was the first to smell the smoke.

Funereal Recollections with a Line from Adrienne Rich

At the wake for her ninety-year-old mother, my childhood friend
confided that they called each other every day of her adult life.

I still hear my own almost forty years beyond
the grave, steel threads unbroken.

I can't hear myself think, she used to cry
against the unrelenting noise of our household.

I so want to tell her I've found a way,
"—a language to hear myself with."
But how would she recognize my voice
if she'd never really heard her own?

Is it true that at the hour of death, mothers mistake
daughters for their own mothers?

Since You Asked

A sunflower, dinner-plate wide, gold face to the sky;
another, head heavy, droops dark to the ground.

An older gentleman, white wine at lunch,
his maroon garden-print cane propped beside him.

Magnificent views from the library's top floor,
but not the sweet, musty smell I went to find.

If only I could tell you.
I couldn't sleep.

Passersby talking—"Judas was a saint, too, you know."
"I'm here, Mom. I'm still on the phone."

A child ringing bells on bicycles locked to the wrought-iron fence.
Shadows on the cobblestone.

Ferry horn sounds deep in the distance.
Pink blouse billowing, a woman paddles her board toward the pier.

Marie said you're not writing the poem,
the poem's writing you.

It's an art, this losing.
I couldn't begin to tell you.

II

Of These Women

Anne O'Malley Holleran, late of County Galway,
my great-grandmother.

Mary Holleran Hyland, my grandmother,
buried her mother and her daughter in Pittsburgh.

Anna Mae Hyland, mother of eight,
my mother, over half my life without her.

Anne, Mary, Anna Mae,
blessed springs, blessed streams.

Jane Anne—
I, the scribe.

Cara Anne, my firstborn,
doctor, wife, mother of one daughter, two sons.

Emma Jane, tall stem of a girl, strong swimmer,
my granddaughter.

Litany is my lineage—
a river within spills light.

The Pontiac

I'm stretched across the back seat
of our family's green sedan,
sliding with each sharp turn
down tree-shrouded streets.
We hit the snaking highway,
headlights cross over my mother,
Grace-Kelly-scarfed,
cigarette-hand on the wheel.

The dingy tunnel, narrow and long,
launches us onto the Liberty Bridge.
I lean against the half-open window and
the stench of rotten eggs fills my nose.
Mountains of coal and iron ore
smolder along the black river's edge.
Mill stacks shoot great orange plumes
into the night.

Mom and I sing
with Doris Day on the radio,
Que Sera, Sera.

Only Child

My parents were great dancers,
but a few rhythmic missteps made
my dad, a devout Catholic
and fatherless only child,
the father of eight.
Each day after grapefruit, toast and coffee,
fedora-topped, he climbed the hill—
the bus downtown and same bus home.
Each evening, they sipped Manhattans
knee to knee; his LP crooners set the mood.
From the head of our crowded dinner table,
he talked of office, city, world, then
retreated from the bedtime chaos to *Advise
and Consent* and *The Cardinal,*
Time, Life and *Cheaper
by the Dozen.*
The eight of us were hers.
I wanted to be his.

Two Women in the House

When Gram moved in, we had two whistling teakettles,
two stout electric mixers, doubles of almost everything.

Mom used a cast iron skillet, Melmac ash trays;
Gram, her silver thimble and bone china teacups.

Gram baked and iced dark chocolate cookies
by the shoebox-full,

but Mom stopped cooking
with Dad's mother in the kitchen.

Cupboards so laden and cramped, and me,
a child between—

Veterans Day

I don't think she ever took me along,
but on this morning every year, I can see
my mother's mother all in black,
the only color I ever saw her wear,
slipping out the back door,
pocketbook on her arm,
and a hat, always a dress hat.

She stands alone at the bus stop, heading
downtown to the corner of Market and Fifth,
to the spot where she watches the parade
of soldiers who returned.
The crowd jostles her tiny frame
but she fights to hold her ground
hugging the curb.

My grandmother studies the faces
of uniformed young men, clear eyes,
ruddy cheeks in the cold November wind.
She searches those faces for hers,
lost New Year's Day of '45,
Sergeant John Joseph Hyland
—her Jack.

Uncle Bud
Thomas Hyland, 1918-1998

No use kicking! you'd say
when we'd ask how you were,
arthritic back, shoulders, neck.
A calendar tacked to the kitchen wall,
you marked anniversaries of deaths:
brother, father, brother, sister, mother, brother.
Jack, the first to go, the only one lost in the war.
On the mantel, his boyish picture:
starched white collar and black robe,
the novitiate at thirteen.

Just days before you died,
you dreamt a football game
at LaSalle in Philadelphia—Jack's
alma mater, not yours. The stadium
packed, the sky clear, the sun bright.
The old man was cheering me on,
cheering like hell! You said
the score board showed a win but
the headlines read: Thomas Hyland is dead.

The stadium still roars down here below.

The Irish Hour

Sunday afternoons at three,
my grandmother cradled
her mug of tea against her heart,
listened to the kitchen radio—

wood flutes, tin whistles
became Galway's far dulcet shores
where she'd traveled once,
green fields, green hills, green prayers.

What did she recall
a girl, just six, clutching her mother's hand?
So many mourners keening
at a family grave.

Snapshot of the Eight of Us

Admonished to stand still
beneath the blazing August sun,
the youngest girl, just three, cries
squirming under Mom's firm grip.

Sentinel in cat-eye glasses on the other end,
I sense my littlest brother's unease
my arm extended, hand cupped
on this tiny twin's shoulder.

The tallest boy is oldest, crewcut,
gold jersey, tight, bicep flexed and
fingers poised to pinch
the ear of the serious, younger one.

Identical fair-haired boys standing
center-front, in Sunday best,
matching blue-collared, striped shirts,
my charges when the second set arrived.

The middle girl, shiny black hair,
her cheeks full, smiles thinly
as if she has a secret—she,
the dancer, the schemer, the clown.

All of us would pose like this
but twice more
before Mom is gone,
and we drift apart.

Crossings

Mom died at home at fifty-four,
died in a rented hospital bed
under the window in the room facing
the master bedroom, bath en suite,
fifth-floor corner condo
in a flat-field suburb south of Chicago.
I remember my two-year old was napping
when Dad called—
She's gone.

fragments left unwritten in my mother's prayer book

I can't tell a soul
        what a relief it is to let go.

     O when the Saints go marching
            we were girls together
   Therese & Patsy   gone.

The doctors blame the cigarettes
I couldn't live without coffee and cigarettes
           Manhattans before dinner.

            The kids are driving me crazy
               stop the fighting
            I don't want any more tears.

Note from My Younger Sister
on the 36th Anniversary of Our Mother's Death

I was so young.
Mom wanted me with her more,
more than ever & I resisted—
I was a teenager
moving away not realizing
the finality of it all.
Oh, to have just a bit of that time back.

I still remember the physical pain
that Sunday. Everyone alone
with the loss, in separate rooms.
Tom had just come home from church.
We were told to stay away, not to watch
her body being removed.

Total Eclipse in Thirty-One Syllables

I recall no spring—
eight of us lost our mother,
Dad, his wife too soon,
your mother, her only daughter,
& you lost us all, at once.

I didn't want to turn away

as the mother robin,
like mothers everywhere—
like my own, stole each swirling
tendril for her gray-streaked bowl.

Feathers coated in pollen, golden-
green, she sat unmoved,
Spring's wild, whistling gusts
rocking the Andromeda bush.

Yet still I wonder for her brood,
at the emptiness of her nest.
Tell me what you told me this morning …
tell me again and again.

III

Passing My Younger Self on the Beach: A Cento

Birds afloat in air's currents
some children run after each other squealing in the shallows
    near but not too near
she seems to want to be both caught and free
—watching rather   the spaces of sand between them

the sun-warmed sand   the surf   this reunion
a to and a from   and an urgency
her mind full to the wind   I see her plunge
return for a snack   with gobbling mother-eye
thinking sweetness sweetness

Three Haiku

vastness of stars
a cold wind
stirs the evergreens

Cold Moon
my daughter cries
as her water breaks

morning sun
the scent of Easter chocolates
with my grandchild's kiss

Mother's Day

Peonies!
I love how they burst
out wide
full beyond
their own brief,
just-lapsed moment.

Falling

I've fallen many times:
the usual stumbles
over secret schoolgirl crushes,
head-over-heels for teen heartthrobs.
I loved them all.

I've fallen so many times:
tripped down the aisle
over husband, daughter, son.
Madly and deeply,
I love them all.

I've fallen again and again:
new friends, a mentor, a muse,
numerous books, a few authors,
four dear pups and a stranger, or two.
I loved them all.

I've fallen farther,
fallen faster,
now captivated, I tumble—
enthralled with my grandchildren.
I love them each, ever and all.

Woman to Woman

There's a funny cartoon in a recent *New Yorker.*
You may have seen it: a man and his therapist,
on each man's head sits an identical owl.

Three stories up, we're in your office overlooking the river,
see a cloud of ruby-throated hummingbirds.
It's different for us—somehow sweeter.

Summer Tanka

Crickets crescendo.
Watercolor black swirling
behind my eyelids.

I'm face-to-face with August,
the night sky's wild abundance.

A New Year's Eve Heart-to-Heart

With toddler pluck, he swings into action.
What are you doing, Ben?
—Climbing on the coffee table.

Squatting, he steadies himself.
What would Mommy say?
—No climbing on the coffee table.

He straightens, as if atop Everest, victorious.
What would Daddy say?
—No climbing on the coffee table.

My red-pajamaed climber surveys the room.
I hover lest he stumble. How will this end?
What does Nana say?

—What are you doing, Ben?
He grins and throws his arms round my neck.
I whirl him, twirl him and we fly.

At Four: A Birth Pantoum

My grandson wants to know about babies.
His sister (and he himself) was once that small
Deep in the mountain of Mommy's belly.
He wonders "how babies get out," that's all.

His sister (and he himself) was once that small,
A tiny creature trapped and kicking.
He wonders "how babies get out," that's all.
"How do doctors do their helping?"

A tiny creature trapped and kicking!
His mother struggles with his inquiry.
"How do doctors do their helping?"
How can she satisfy his curiosity?

His mother struggles with his inquiry.
"Through the birth canal, that's it."
How can she satisfy his curiosity?
"What's a canal?" "A waterway." She's quick.

Through the birth canal. That's it.

"Babies can't swim. The birth canal?" he resists.

"What's a canal?" "It's a waterway!" She's quick.

"Is it on the side or back?" His questioning persists.

"Babies can't swim. The birth canal?" he resists.

Deep in the mountain of Mommy's belly,

"Is it on the side or back?" His questioning persists.

My grandson wants to know about babies.

Star Wars

Sunday at dinner,

Ben talks of Ms. Vader,

one of the second-grade teachers.

I hope her first name isn't Darth.

Dad scores a few chuckles.

Emma, proud kindergartener,

looks up at her brother.

Her name is Ella,

Ella Vader.

From deep in her belly,

a long, satisfied giggle.

Smartphone Photos of My Granddaughter

Though I decry the ubiquity
of technology in children's lives,

I delight as Emma comes into focus
in my daughter's eye—

beaming in her birthday crown
crafted on the last day of kindergarten

balancing on her dad's shoulders
about to dive into Owl Pond,

cart-wheeling between her brothers' soccer balls
across the sweet green carpet of June.

In these snapshots, Emma has yet to take
hip hop classes or join the Bluefish swim team

nor has she designed Bitmojis in her own image,
long dark hair with her arms wide open, and one in mine,

signature cat-eye glasses, to send back and forth
full of hearts and balloons on random occasions, until,

in an instant, she's holding her own phone, swept up
with BFFs and the middle school social scene.

Barbie At Rest

A little girl & her grandmother have taken me
across an unfamiliar threshold.
They pose me in Downward Facing Dog,
Arm Balance, Head Stand & Corpse.
Like many late middle-agers,
with stiff ankles, knees, hips,
I've danced & skated, skied & run,
over-trained, for sure. I've walked endless
runways in ridiculously high heels.
But when the girl stretches me out flat,
my back & legs settle into the wooden floor,
tears flow down my cheeks, puddle in my ears,
& I go where I've never been before—

Triumphant Conquest

At thirteen months,
the day after his first
two steps alone,
Jake spotted another child's
castle of wooden blocks
on the purple rug
in his big brother's
first-grade classroom.
Letting go of my hand,
Jake took five steps, six,
reached the coveted construction
and snatched the triangle
perched atop the tower.
Neither toppled.

Buon Compleanno

Ding, dong. Pizza! Pizza man. Two-year-old Jake shouts and races away from the front door. Hold me, he cries, leaping into his Papa's arms. Jake watches intently from a safe distance as the gray-haired delivery man slides three large cardboard boxes out of the bright red insulated sleeve onto the kitchen counter. Steamy, hot pies for our family gathering. The cheery visitor pulls a much smaller box out of his coat pocket, lifts his arms like wings and, then, breathes into his shiny harmonica— Happy birthday to you!

April's evening chill
Sweet serenade transports us—
In Italia

Sudden Downpour

Three-year old Jake & I ran
through the pouring rain.
What will Mommy say?
he laughed & laughed.
Under a neighbor's tree, we stopped
to watch water stream down
the cracked sidewalk
forming a puddle.
Jake splashed with abandon,
sneakers sopping.
What will Mommy say?
All his clothes soaking wet—
except his big-boy pants.
What will Mommy say!

Candy Land at Four: A Pantoum

OH, MAN! Jake's voice like thunder,
he drags his token to Gingerbread Man.
Did you shuffle these cards? Glummer,
he's back where he first began.

He drags his token to Gingerbread Man
far from Queen Frostine's Lake.
Back where he first began—Nana,
we'll never get out of this game!

Far from Queen Frostine's Lake,
Jake warns me of dangers that lurk.
Nana, we'll never get out of this game!
On Lord Licorice, I lose my next turn.

Jake warns me that dangers lurk.
He plays steadily, one purple, two blues.
Oh, no, Lord Licorice! I miss another turn.
Maybe I'll get Gumdrop Pass, he muses.

He persists as I tire: one yellow, two blues.

I advance only one space each go.

Maybe I'll get Gramma Nut, he amuses,

sliding my token; I'm slow.

Can it be—only one space each go?

Did you shuffle these cards? Jake grins.

His spirit and spunk move me so.

OH, MAN! Jake laughs. And he wins!

Demeter to Her Eight-Year-Old Granddaughter

You're not mine for long—
August sweeps the dunes and
your mother prepares to leave,
but, here beside the water,
I watch you
dig and pack wet sand,
tenderly place speckled stones
& blue-black mussel shells
on your proud afternoon castle.

My Poet's Eye at Dusk

Driving home from a movie
and early supper, Papa and I
slowed for a shimmery-tailed fox,
steady, confident stride,
crossing Old King's Highway,
dinner dangling from its mouth.
His, hers, who knows?
Aren't we all the same,
seekers of sustenance
in this abundant season—
blue bulbous hydrangea,
arching vermillion lilies,
layers and layers of green
as July's silver light
thins to gray.

An Ordinary Day

It happened on a corner
I never imagined—
stepping down off the curb
my grandson untangled our fingers
and locked his arm
full round mine,
lest I fall.

IV

Conjunctions

I watch the sparrows flit
from branch to branch
beneath the half-full feeder.

A bird on Dickinson's walk,
flash of white through hemlock hedge,
I see her offering a crumb.

With bread and worms failing,
I tiptoed behind a robin, my hands
cupping a mound of table salt.

I must have been quite young,
my mother tolerated no such nonsense
once there were eight of us.

Oh, to have one
of my own, its heartbeat
on my shoulder.

A flurry of sparrows skitter,
skirmish. From where I sit,
their rivalries so small.

Seasons later, do birds
perched on snowy branches
recognize nest mates?

Wings unfurl
the Soul unto itself—
in Awe.

Lost Ground

Jill McLean Taylor 1944-2010

My friend died suddenly.
No psalm nor prayer
can console.

Her vibrancy stilled in old photos.
Her voice pressed between pages
stacked on library shelves.

Fall's foliage fell abruptly.
Black branches, knots exposed,
wet leaves amassed below.

Her husband curses his fate.
Her sons swaddle sorrow in humor.
And the bells toll noon.

Mainz, Thanksgiving Week, 2014

Bone-weary from the overnight flight, my husband and I trail behind
our son, who took the first train to meet us at the Frankfurt airport. The
Sunday morning silence dwarfs the clatter of our suitcases across the
dawn-damp cobblestones.

Old meets new across the millennia in this place once conquered by
the Romans, occupied by Napoleon's troops and bombed by the Allies.
I find a beauty and grit in the restorations, a tolerance for glass facades
attached to centuries-old stone walls.

Tim studied abroad many times and we visited, but this is different. A
teaching job at the university made this small city in Germany his new
home.

Had I been careless in what I wished for?

> The Rhine's foggy breath
> dove gray to silvery white
> accommodates

To The Season

I'll not be sending
festive cards and photos
with red and green stamps.
I'll not be writing long letters,
in cursive strokes and swirls
of ivy and mistletoe,
though I may wish I had.

December, O December,
as your days and nights
unfold, I'm drawn to dwell
in your cold, clear stillness,
in your brief, singular light.

Pacific Time

Jet-lagged and bleary-eyed,
on that January morning
I wasn't prepared for warm
breezes, soft California skies,
the pastel, sun-shiny nursing home
(in Carlsbad of all cities,
you loved so many others,
Pittsburgh, Chicago, New York).
Your sensible second wife, Mary,
had to move you there.

Dad, it was your watch that
caught my attention,
the large, simple face of it,
the stretch-gold band
you always wore, by then
loose on your frail wrist,
bare arm fully exposed
by the hospital Johnny.

Father of eight, only three
at your bedside near the end.
Mary was thought to be crying wolf.
You, so clear-headed, scolding us
I gave you directions. What the hell
took you so long?

We ended up laughing
about the old cast of parish priests,
their homilies. You hadn't been
to church in the twenty years
since Mom's death,
but you were relieved to have
a plan— we'd take you back
east for mass at St. Paul's
where you & Mom married in '47,
back to her grave at Calvary.
The weekend passed quickly.
My tears were too few.

With your watch and your wits,
you died alone a few weeks later.

Snowstorm After Snowstorm

Trash barrels and rosebushes

alike, buried in what feels

like catastrophe.

I count five cardinals

crisscrossing the backyard tundra.

Vespers red, lights deep

in the spindly hedge— one stays

as if in meditation—

why this chasing of days.

Overdue

if I were writing this
into daylight
freedom's plow
carry the one

how her spirit got out
hot milk
the flashboat
mysticism for beginners

the rest of life
shoes outside the door
stargazer's sister
hurt into beauty

Bus Stop in the January Rain

No umbrella   her head draped
loosely in a red-print scarf
hijab perhaps I don't know
she checks her app   It's coming
four more minutes
On the crowded bus   we sit
talk together   her job
search   my son teaching
in Germany   her falling
in love in France   his move
to Russia   the election
our fears   her wish to live
nearer to her elderly father
at the station   we part

The Landscape Listens

At this conference honoring women poets,
 a man, one of many invited
to preside at the podium,
casually called Adrienne Rich's later work,
"strange."
A rumbling restlessness
stirred in the audience.
A woman stood up,
I recall her words now,
She saved my life—

Pose

My yoga teacher says to notice
the space between my right earlobe
and right shoulder, left earlobe and left shoulder.

--my hair is clipped so close to my head,
I'm all but bald.

I trace a line from the top of my head through
the roof of my mouth
down to my tailbone.

Dreaded pixie cut of my youth,
I feel my cheeks flush.

I stand fingertips reaching,
raised eyebrows and spreading collar bones.
My shoulder blades settle.

This haircut conjures terrors, I have,
thus far, been spared.

Beneath my exposed scalp,
I turn inward and silence
familiar sirens.

Mountain on a cloudless day,
feet rooted.

Passages

Lone hours pass unsung

down crowded city streets,

while others rush by, colorful

scarves trailing in the wind.

Hours heavy with worry lag

storm after storm.

Some arrive, full backpacks

open on the family table.

Endless, empty hours lie

graveled in grief.

In evening's lamp light,

a lull & you return,

as in the beginning,

your breath in my ear.

March

Mounds of fresh wood chips

lie in piles around the pond

like Monet's haystacks of sun and season.

In entryways of markets and the station,

winter tulips

forced pink into red—

we humans of such spare beauty,

kiss them with lips of vases, scatter

their pollen on linen cloths.

Tall, spindly, let

pines redress the light.

Easter, 2020

As Nature shouts alleluias,

choruses of daffodils & birdsong,

in this moment, what words

can express the feeling—

my chest filling-and-collapsing

all at once

as if I've returned

from the dead &

catch your eye

but can't touch you.

Map of a Reluctant Requiem

For Stephen Bresnahan, M.D. Geriatrician, 1956-2019

St. Agatha's of Quincy & Milton,
crowded wooden pews, long, creaky kneelers,
I sit with my daughter in disbelief.

A solemn procession—Jocelyn & the kids,
elderly priests in white cotton cassocks.
No coffin at the foot of the altar.

Gothic grandeur in summer's early light,
your heart beats deep within this gathering,
in your green-canopied home state,

across the blue-bright Atlantic waters,

near to your beloved Haitian patients

at the mountain clinic of St. Rock.

No body, no blood.
You remain.

V

In Praise of the Older Women at Water Aerobics

When I first splashed into the sparkling water

with all of you, my seniors by near decades,

I saw your smart, black bathing suits,

coifed crowns of tinted brown or gray,

some snapped into latex caps.

You stirred strong currents then, on cue,

reversed direction, inhaling laughter,

exhaling all your bluesy aches.

Oh, sister selkies, I still bob in

the buoyancy of your circle.

Scarred replacement knees, bald spots,

occasional red lipstick and funky plastic shades—

I delight in your aquatic ballet teaching me

to love old women, to love

the one I'm becoming.

Alone in the House

Sorting through clothes

you'd left behind

when you headed for college,

it was your name

embroidered on the jacket sleeve,

gold thread on royal blue corduroy,

that stirred a familiar pang—

hugging you, my chin resting

on the top of your head.

       I carefully folded and

packed boyhood into the box

for Goodwill.

It Wasn't A Dream

With champagne-colored wings,

you burrowed through

my winter woolens, ravenous

for sweaty seams and stains.

Crawling with charm and humor,

you tickled out my disavowed desires.

The closet door ajar, you escaped

into the streaming light

to seek others' hidden wardrobes.

Telltale marks of your prodding

on the sleeve of my blue sweater.

I remember how you loved

used things—

I wanted to be new.

Sunday Afternoon at Alabama Jack's

Driving to Key West, sun hot and high, we pulled up to the "must-see"
open-air bar,
a tin roof joint on a barge in the green waters of the Everglades.

On the crowded dance floor, we were surrounded by bikers and
snowbird couples who two-stepped, sashayed to a crazy-country beat
— *Rockin' Robin, Mama Said, Please Mister Postman.*

I noticed her dancing alone, tall and willowy, soft, yellow flounced
skirt, unadorned, dusty-brown cowboy boots.

She tilted her head, swinging her long, gray hair.
I took that sweet solitude home.

A Teacher in Every Gun Shop

— a bold bumper sticker

on a beat-up Ford.

Missives that call us out:

Black Lives Matter

surrounded by too many

tiny red flags on the First Church lawn.

Heed that teacher:

use your words.

Bookends

Jenny erect in the wing-back chair
a walker parked in front of her

Ellie in her wheelchair elbows wide
fingers intertwined as if in prayer

daughters of immigrants East Boston housewife
college professor from Brooklyn —

between them almost one hundred and eighty-four years
two first husbands a second and a third

three daughters three sons two houses
one dog and many good friends

Jenny talking on and on about the way things were
Ellie listening her words often melting before she can speak

Jenny claims she never ever swore but once
her husband made her so mad she yelled: BITCH!

I think that would be Bastard Ellie's face
glows with her succinct conclusion.

Dwelling

Eleanor H, Chasdi, Ph.D. 1927-2018

Arriving at the home to visit, I hear you.
I'm waiting for the bus to Brooklyn.
You want to see your family—

your father, proud member
of the Workmen's Circle
in the new country, your mother,

worried housewife, with her late life
daughter, your little sister, at her side.
It's not home, this place where you wait.

I feel like you know who I am.
When words won't come,
your eyes soften, a certain smile.

Sometimes you introduce me to a nurse,
This is Jane. My friend, Jane.
And you, my friend and mentor still.

Mine's the pleasure of announcing
your son David's coming from Berlin.
I can repeat that message

five or six times in an hour.
You reply, *Oh, I didn't know that.
Good, good, good.*

Around the table, a few stare silently.
One greets everybody with *I love you,*
another chants *bitch, bitch, bitch.*

Onto the red brick patio, I wheel you,
Ellie, cocooned in a blanket
against November's chill, full-face

to the sun, swirling surround of gold
ornamental grasses and nearly pink
yellow leaves flying above. You reach

for dusty-purple hydrangeas nestled
beside the six-story building.
Once again, you ask where we are.

For My Son and His Bride: An Abecedarian

All is joy
Bold red ribbons and lights of
Christkindlmarkt Wiesbaden
Dear new daughter in white suit and stole
Exuberant son in a gray fedora
Facing the well-wishers who gather

Glühwein in bright ceramic mugs
Hail the love you've found together
Its intimacy   its wonder
Justine and Tim
Know mystery and melody
Let laughter and sympathy sustain you
May you prosper and may
No troubles cloud your new horizons
Only soft sunlight on your path   I pray

People near the carousel strain to watch
Queue sideways as you pass
Remember this moment   its fullness
Savor its sweetness   its tang—
Trust yourselves   the ground beneath you
United in matrimony
Vows spoken each to each
Widening circles of merriment rise
X, Y, Zinging…all is joy.

Nearing Our 39th Anniversary

I dream I'm writing you
a blue-green poem,
open sky, new leaves, sparkling
blades of grass.
I write and rewrite, refine
its cadence and rhythm.
I type and retype so as to
memorize its contours,
short lines in Arial font.
Then I wake to the dawn ceiling,
your staccato snoring, sprawling
leg across mine.

not lost on the hummingbirds

from three scraggly geraniums

last ones left on the sale rack,

John's pick, despite my pique,

plopped into a plastic pot

of last season's soil,

fertilized, watered & sunned—

riotous July bouquet.

VI

Autumn Ghazal

Climbing the wall of my beloved, second-bloom garden,
roses, pink, red and rogue in this late-afternoon garden.

Perhaps no greater joy, astonishing emergence—
no as-in-the-beginning, fruit blossom June garden.

Red-clapboard library, bright against early nightfall,
beloved old picture books, stuffed animal strewn garden.

Like a Rothko chapel, color drenched space, bamboo floor,
scent of cinnamon— tree, warrior, half-moon garden.

November foliage falls suddenly, branches exposed,
wet leaves amassing, bells toll funereal noon garden.

The neighbor's kind old mutt howls a swelling sadness,
dappled moonlight shines through thinning oaks—Jane's rune garden.

Questions

Did your mother look Irish?
With no trace of a smile,
the woman poet, visiting from Dublin,
 scanned my face.
What was her maiden name?
Hyland, I replied.
Ah, not a very common name back home.
What border did she guard
persisting in her interrogation,
as I argued my long-dead mother and her
predecessors back through the port of Cobh,
into the purple-blue hills of Connemara—
their wild, hungry Beauty.

Stars

Glenn Close, Viola Davis, Bette Midler—
my sister, Jackie, has a long list of celebrities
she's met in the rush & bustle of her annual trips
to New York City with her husband.
In Takashimaya Midtown, she spotted Meryl Streep
in the first floor garden. As Jackie tells it,
She saw me and looked scared I was going
to approach. Which, of course, I was.
I stopped myself when I saw her face.
She slipped out the revolving door.

I wonder if Jackie sometimes searches
for our mother in crowds, like I do—
Mom on her honeymoon with Dad
in Times Square, Mom smoking alone
as he tries to hail a cab, Mom climbing
the steps of St. Patrick's Cathedral.
If she could come back to life,
for even the briefest moment,
what unexpected terror of recognition,
ache of the light.

Natural History

As the congregation of meadow birds dwindles,
I'm drawn to watch them, in ones or twos,
slice the harvest gray air, goldenrods
unfurling and brittle-brown
Queen Anne's Lace bowing low.

Anne, my mother, long-deceased,
steadfast resurrection-of-the-body-
life-everlasting kind of faith;
my own stitched with awe & doubt
in these dark November days
of threatened catastrophe.

Lithe winged descendants of dinosaurs,
fall birds stir hope and cold conclusions.
Who will survive our reckless Anthropocene?
Wild carrots sweep the path.

the future is a desperate midwife

At seventy, I can't begin to tell you—

mountains of oatmeal, almonds, avocadoes

& extra- virgin olive oil with greens, greens, greens—

my astonishment that the twenty-fifth reunion was

twenty-five years ago, my grandkids now on the runway

of their own second decade. Oh, so many secular psalms

read in amber tones for too many who once were close.

Senses waning, how close my surrender of car keys,

the unmarked turn off the grid.

Daffodils thrash & trumpet through

cacophonous downpours, beg equanimity

& strength—eagle, warrior & sphinx.

If only I could tell you how fierce

my aversion to horizons.

Epilogue: A Cento

I was the first to smell the smoke
I couldn't begin to tell you—
at a family grave
a child between
accommodates

I don't want any more tears
que sera, sera
once again you ask where we are
the night's wild abundance
& I go where I've never been before

why this chasing of days
I wanted to be new
your breath in my ear
ache of the light.

Notes

"Funereal Recollections with a Line from Adrienne Rich" uses the line, "—a language to hear myself with," from Rich's poem, "Tear Gas," 1969.

"The Irish Hour" takes its name from a radio program in the 1950's.

"Passing My Younger Self on the Beach" is a cento, composed with passages from other poets. In this case, line by line, the poets are: Denise Levertov, Marie Howe, Elizabeth Bishop, Anna DiMartino, Gail Mazur, Brenda Shaughnessy, Adrienne Rich, Gwendolyn Brooks and Sylvia Plath.

"An Ordinary Day" won the Sidewalk Poetry contest and is engraved in the sidewalk on Walnut Street in Newtonville, MA.

"Conjunctions" ends with lines from Emily Dickinson (683). An earlier version of this poem won the New England Poetry Club Barbara Bradley Award in 2014.

"Overdue" is a found poem composed of titles of books on my desk.

Authors in order of appearance: Robert Creeley, Jeffrey Harrison, Theresa Perry, Carol Anshaw, Krysten Hill, Deborah Levy, Jane Cooper, Adam Zagajewski, Mary Gordon, Michael Downing, Carrie Brown, Paul Hostovsky.

"The Landscape Listens" is the name of a conference honoring great American women poets, (March 21, 2014, Boston University) and is borrowed from a line in Dickinson (258).

In "Natural History," I refer to Queen Anne's Lace and wild carrots, two names for Daucus carota, a biennial plant, whose flowers resemble lace and whose roots resemble edible carrots. Originating in Northern Europe and Asia, the plant was naturalized to North America, where it's referred to as a weed, beneficial by some and noxious by others.

"Epilogue" is a cento, composed of last lines from poems in this collection.

Acknowledgements

I am grateful to the editors of the following journals where these poems appeared, some in slightly different versions:

The Aurorean: "Summer Tanka"; "Smartphone Photos of My Granddaughter"; "To the Season"

Bird's Thumb: "In Praise of the Older Women at Water Aerobics"

Blast Furnace: "3725 Frazier Street, 1965"; "Pontiac"; "At Four: A Birth Pantoum"

Boston Literary Magazine: "New Year's Eve Heart-to Heart"; "Triumphant Conquest"

Common Ground Review: "It Wasn't A Dream"

Earth's Daughter: "Veterans Day"

Haibun Today: "Mainz: Thanksgiving Week, 2014"

Halfway Down the Stairs: "The Irish Hour"; "Questions"; "Pose"; "Total Eclipse in Thirty-One Syllables"

Ink, Sweat and Tears: "Three Haiku"

Isacoustic: "My Poet's Eye"; "Stars"

Mom Egg Review: "Passing My Younger Self on the Beach"

Muddy River Poetry Review: "Pacific Time"

Off the Coast: "The Landscape Listens"

Pittsburgh Poetry Review: "Funereal Recollections with a Line from Adrienne Rich"

poems2go: "An Ordinary Day"

Poetry Breakfast: "Since You Asked"

Poetry Quarterly: "Snapshot of the Eight of Us"

Rat's Ass Review: "Bus Stop in the January Rain"; "I didn't want to turn away"

Right Hand Pointing: "Star Wars"

Still Crazy: "Only Child"; "Alone in the House"; "Sunday Afternoon at Alabama Jack's"

The Sunlight Press Literary Journal: "Dwelling"; "Bookends"; "Demeter to her Eight-Year-Old Granddaughter"

Thrush Poetry Journal: "the future is a desperate midwife"

Tipton Poetry Review: "Natural History"

TRIVIA: Voices of Feminism: "Barbie at Rest"

UnLost Journal: "Overdue"

The Writer's Almanac: "Falling"

I extend my heartfelt gratitude to my teachers David Semanki, Marie Howe, Gail Mazur, Brenda Shaughnessy and Daniel Johnson who guided me in poetry workshops at the Cambridge Center for Adult Education in Cambridge, the Fine Arts Work Center in Provincetown and Grub Street in Boston. I especially want to thank the readers of my poems for their careful attention and insights: Dianne Argyris, Nina Avedon, Cynthia Bargar, Jay Boulanger, Mary Buchinger, Merrill Douglas, Michael Downing, Wendy Drexler, Mark Jensen, Victoria Korth, Florence Ladd, Charlotte Pence and Marjorie Thomsen. Special thanks to editor, Kevin Walzer, for consistent and concise responses to my questions.

With unwavering support from my husband, John, and with the encouragement of our children, Cara and Tim, my writing grows. Our grandchildren, Ben, Emma and Jake, have been sustaining muses. My daughter-in-law, Justine, was ever-available as editor and computer advisor. She introduced me to my cover artist, Margot Breuer and cover designer, Johanne Breuer. Their artistry releases the light of my poems into the world.

About the Cover Artist

Margot Zündorf Breuer was born in Rheine, Germany, in 1960. After training as a carpenter, she studied product design and graphic design / visual communication at the Münster University of Applied Sciences, graduating in 1987. Since then, she has worked as a freelance artist. In 1996 she moved to Finland. In Espoo, Jyväskylä, and Helsinki, she created numerous works inspired by the Finnish landscape and Finnish culture in both form and content. In 2006 she returned to Germany. She is based in Mainz, where she has created her most important works to date, partly in cooperation with the sculptor Regina Zapp.

Margot Zündorf Breuer is a member of the Federal Associations of Visual Artists (*Bundesverbände Bildender KünstlerInnen*) in Rhineland-Palatinate and Saarland.

The image featured on the cover is Zündorf Breuer's "Sun Spirits of Time with Boat" (*Sonnengeister der Zeit mit Boot*, mixed media on canvas, 2019).

Zündorf Breuer has described her artistic motivation as follows:

My work is about boundaries: in other words, spaces of transition or liminal zones. For me, boundaries are never fixed, but always in flux, changeable, and open. […] I work on the shift and dissolution of visual expectations and address the contingency, fragility, and indecipherability of current forms of life.

mail@margot-zuendorf-breuer.de
www.margot-zuendorf-breuer.de

About the Author

Jane Attanucci grew up in Pittsburgh, Pennsylvania and moved to Boston to attend Emmanuel College. She holds an Ed.D. in Human Development from Harvard Graduate School of Education. After a career in college teaching and research, she studied poetry at the Cambridge Center for Adult Education and the Fine Arts Work Center in Provincetown, Massachusetts. Attanucci's poems have appeared in *Common Ground Review, Off the Coast, Pittsburgh Poetry Review, Third Wednesday, Thrush Poetry Journal* and *Writer's Almanac* among others. She was awarded the New England Poetry Club's Barbara Bradley Award in 2014. Her chapbook, *First Mud,* was released by Finishing Line Press in 2015. She lives in Cambridge, Massachusetts.

Made in the USA
Monee, IL
21 October 2021